MW01520643

6 Studies for Individuals or Groups

Receiving Comfort *from God*

[DALE & JUANITA RYAN]

Letting God Be God Bible Studies

InterVarsity Press
Downers Grove, Illinois

InterVarsity Press
P.O. Box 1400, Downers Grove, IL 60515
World Wide Web: www.ivpress.com
E-mail: mail@ivpress.com

*InterVarsity Press® is the book-publishing division of InterVarsity Christian Fellowship/USA®, a student
movement active on campus at hundreds of universities, colleges and schools of nursing in the United
States of America, and a member movement of the International Fellowship of Evangelical Students.
For information about local and regional activities, write Public Relations Dept., InterVarsity
Christian Fellowship/USA, 6400 Schroeder Rd., P.O. Box 7895, Madison, WI 53707-7895.*

Cover photograph: Michael Goss

Logo and interior icons: Roberta Polfus

ISBN 0-8308-2072-8

Printed in the United States of America ∞

19	18	17	16	15	14	13	12	11	10	9	8	7	6	5	4	3	2	1
16	15	14	13	12	11	10	09	08	07	06	05	04	03	02	01			

CONTENTS

Introduction: Receiving Comfort from God

The LORD is close to the brokenhearted
and saves those who are crushed in spirit.
(Psalm 34:18)

There are times in our lives, many times, when we experience losses of one kind or another. Sometimes the loss we face is small; sometimes it is devastatingly huge. Sometimes the loss is one we have anticipated; sometimes it is a complete surprise. Sometimes loss comes as a result of positive changes. Sometimes there is nothing positive at all. But whatever the loss may be, when we experience loss, we need comfort.

Comfort is the experience of gaining increased strength and hope in the face of grief or distress. This increased strength and hope come from the loving presence of a person who recognizes the distress we are experiencing, feels compassion for our suffering and reaches out in a way that is responsive to our needs. For example, a parent might comfort a frightened child by holding the child, by rocking the child and by talking calmly to the child. Or a friend might comfort us when we are distressed with a hug or by sitting with us and listening respectfully to whatever we need to say.

According to the Bible, God is the "Father of compassion and the God of all comfort, who comforts us in all our troubles" (2 Corinthians 1:3-4). God actively seeks to comfort us. To receive comfort from God is to let God be present with us during our times of distress. It is to let God sit next to us and listen to whatever we need to say; it is to let God hold us and remind us that we are loved, valued and not alone. "Letting God be God" means letting God give himself to us as our comfort in times of loss and distress.

Even though we know that we need comfort from God, we may find ourselves rejecting God's comfort. Sometimes we reject comfort because our grief is too raw, our pain too overwhelming. Sometimes we reject comfort because we need time to protest the injustice of what has happened to us. At other times we may find ourselves resistant to seeking comfort because acknowledging our need for comfort exposes our vulnerability. We may feel an increased need to seem tough or self-sufficient, to protect ourselves from exposure. We may find ourselves saying, "I don't need any help"—just when we need help the most!

Fortunately, God understands the rejection of comfort. God does not hurry us or force comfort on us. God knows we can grow in our capacity to receive comfort.

The studies in this guide are designed to help you open your heart and life to the God of all comfort. It is our prayer that in the process of working through these studies, God's Spirit will free you to receive comfort from God in new ways.

Learning to Let God Be God

The Bible studies in this series are based on three basic convictions. The first of these convictions is that we are by our very nature dependent on our Maker. We need God. We need God's help with the daily challenges of life. We need God's love, peace, forgiveness, guidance and hope. The invitation to "let God be God" is an invitation to let God be who God really is. But it is also an invitation to us to be who we really are—God's deeply loved children.

Second, these studies are based on the conviction that God is willing, ready and eager to be God in our lives. God is not distant, inaccessible or indifferent. Rather, God is actively involved, offering us all that we need. God offers us all the love, strength, hope and peace we need.

Finally, these studies are based on the conviction that the spiritual life begins with receiving from God. What we do when we "let God be God" is receive from God the good gifts that God is eager to give to us. God has offered to love us. We are "letting God be God" when we receive this love. God has offered to guide us. We are "letting God be God" when we receive this guidance. Receiving from God is the starting point of the spiritual life. There is, of course, a place in the Christian journey for giving to God—a place for commitment and dedication. But if we have not learned well to receive from God, then we will almost certainly experience the Christian journey to be full of heavy burdens.

These are basic Christian convictions that closely resemble the first three steps of the twelve steps of Alcoholics Anonymous. The short summary is "I can't. God can. I'll let him." These are spiritual truths that apply to all of our lives. They may seem pretty simple. But most of us find that actually doing them—putting these truths into practice—is anything but simple. The problem is that receiving is not instinctive for most of us. What is instinctive is self-sufficiency, independence and managing by ourselves. What comes naturally is trying harder and trying our hardest. Letting go of this performance-oriented spirituality and allowing ourselves to receive from God will be a challenging adventure for most of us. It is the adventure that is at the heart of these Bible studies.

These Bible studies are designed to help you explore what it means to receive from God—what it means to let God be God in your life. George MacDonald used a wonderful metaphor when talking about the process of learning to receive from God. He said, "There are good things God must delay giving, until his child has a pocket to hold them—until God gets his child to make that pocket" (as cited in Michael R. Phillips, ed., *Discovering the Character of God* [Minneapolis: Bethany House, 1989], p. 156). These studies are designed to help you sew some new pockets that are big enough to hold the abundant good gifts that God has prepared for you.

Getting the Most from These Studies

The guides in this series are designed to assist you to find out what the Bible has to say about God and to grow in your ability to "let God be God" in your life. The passages you study will be thought provoking, challenging, inspiring and very personal. It will become obvious that these studies are not designed merely to convince you of the truthfulness of some idea. And they won't provide a systematic presentation of everything the Bible says about any subject. Rather, they will create an opportunity for biblical truths to renew your heart and mind.

There are six studies in each guide. Our hope is that this will provide you with maximum flexibility in how you use these guides. Combining the guides in various ways will allow you to adapt them to your time schedule and to focus on the concerns most important to you or your group.

All of the studies in this series use a workbook format. Space is provided for writing responses to each question. This is ideal for personal study and allows group members to prepare in advance for the discussion. The guides also contain notes with suggestions on how to lead a group discussion. The notes provide additional background information on certain questions, give helpful tips on group dynamics and suggest ways to deal with problems that may arise during the discussion. These features equip someone with little or no experience to lead an effective discussion.

Suggestions for Individual Study

1. As you begin each study, pray that God would give you wisdom and courage through his Word.

2. After spending time in preparation, read and reread the passage to be studied.

3. Write your responses in the space provided or in a personal journal. Writing can bring clarity and deeper understanding of yourself and God's Word. For the same reason, we suggest that you write out your prayers at various points in each study.

4. Most of the studies include questions that invite you to spend time in meditative prayer. The biblical text is communication addressed personally to us. Meditative prayer can enrich and deepen your experience of a biblical text.

5. After you have completed your study of the passage, you might want to read the leader's notes at the back of the guide to gain additional insight and information.

6. Share what you are learning with someone you trust. If you are not able to use these guides in a group you might want to consider participating in one of our online discussion groups at <www.lettinggodbegod.com>.

Suggestions for Group Study

Even if you have already done these studies individually, we strongly encourage you to find some way to do them with a group of other people as well. Although each person's journey is different, everyone's journey is empowered by the mutual support and encouragement that can only be found in a one-on-one or group setting. Several reminders may be helpful for participants in a group study.

1. Trust grows over time. If opening up in a group setting feels risky, realize that you do not have to share more than what feels safe to you. However, taking risks is a necessary part of growth. So do participate in the discussion as much as you are able.

2. Be sensitive to the other members of the group. Listen attentively when they talk. You will learn from their insights. If you can, link what you say to the comments of others so the group stays on the topic.

3. Be careful not to dominate the discussion. We are sometimes so eager to share what we have learned that we do not leave opportunity for others to respond. By all means participate! But allow others to do so as well.

4. Expect God to teach you through the passage being discussed and through the other members of the group. Pray that you will have a profitable time together.

5. We recommend that groups follow a few basic guidelines and that these guidelines be read at the beginning of each discussion session. The guidelines, which you may wish to adapt to your situation, are

☐ Anything said in the group is considered confidential and will not be discussed outside the group unless specific permission is given to do so.

☐ We will provide time for each person present to talk if he or she feels comfortable doing so.

☐ We will talk about ourselves and our own situations, avoiding conversation about other people.

☐ We will listen attentively to each other.

☐ We will be very cautious about giving advice.

☐ We will pray for each other.

If you are the discussion leader, you will find additional suggestions and helpful ideas for each study in the leader's notes. These are found at the back of the guide.

You might also want to consider participating in the online discussion forum for group leaders at <www.lettinggodbegod.com>.

The Promise of Comfort

ISAIAH 61:1-3

There are times in all of our lives when we experience loss and need to be comforted. We may lose our job. Or a relationship. Or a dream. Or a loved one. During any season of loss and grief, we may feel afraid, powerless and alone. What we need most during these times is to be comforted. We need the strength and hope that come from knowing deeply that we are not alone—from knowing that the God of all comfort has promised to be present with us in times of loss.

The text for this study is a selection from the Old Testament that Jesus read publicly in the synagogue at the beginning of his ministry. It was a kind of purpose statement for his ministry. The text reminds us in dramatic images that the God of all comfort understands our grief and longs to comfort us with tender, powerful love.

PREPARE
What images come to your mind when you think of the word *comfort?*

What are you hoping to receive as you use these studies to explore God's role as a giver of comfort?

READ

¹The Spirit of the Sovereign LORD is on me,
*   because the LORD has anointed me*
*   to preach good news to the poor.*
He has sent me to bind up the brokenhearted,
*   to proclaim freedom for the captives*
*   and release from darkness for the prisoners,*
²to proclaim the year of the LORD's favor
*   and the day of vengeance of our God,*
to comfort all who mourn,
³   and provide for those who grieve in Zion—
to bestow on them a crown of beauty
*   instead of ashes,*
the oil of gladness
*   instead of mourning,*
and a garment of praise
*   instead of a spirit of despair.*
They will be called oaks of righteousness,
*   a planting of the LORD*
*   for the display of his splendor. (Isaiah 61:1-3)*

STUDY

1. What would be a good title for this text?

2. According to this text, what categories of people is God hoping to reach with the good news?

---

3. Which of these categories do you identify with the most?

---

4. List the comforting actions that are promised in verses 1 and 2.

---

5. God is reaching out to comfort us in these ways. How do these images of a God who comforts compare with your personal experience of God?

---

6. Verse 3 describes grief using images of ashes, mourning and despair. What does God promise to do in order to comfort people who are grieving?

7. In a moment of quiet, picture yourself being comforted in these ways by God. Write about what you experience.

---

8. The final image in this text is an image of strength. Read this image, personalizing it with your name. What response do you have to the promise of being strengthened by God in this way?

---

9. What kind of comfort do you need at this time?

REFLECT
Read Matthew 11:28-30. Allow yourself to hear this direct invitation from Jesus to come with your burdens. Write about your honest response to this invitation.

RESPOND
Reread this text from Isaiah every day this week. Let the images and promises speak to you in your specific situation. Keep a journal of your responses to each day's reading.

2

Refusing God's Comfort

PSALM 77

It doesn't make much sense to refuse comfort. But many of us do it all the time. It may be that we think we don't deserve to be comforted. Or we may think that we are not supposed to need comfort—that we are supposed to be strong on our own. Or we may see true comfort as too much to hope for. These are just some of the thoughts which may confuse us in times when we need comfort. We may not even know that we are thinking things like this. But it is such thoughts that lead us to refuse comfort when we need it the most.

God wants to comfort us. God has promised to comfort us. The text for this study can help us face our fears about being comforted. It shows us a way to move through these fears so that we can open our hearts to God's comforting presence.

 PREPARE

When you think about being comforted during a time of distress, what fears are you aware of?

When you think about being comforted during a time of distress, what hopes are you aware of?

READ

> [1]*I cried out to God for help;*
>   *I cried out to God to hear me.*
> [2]*When I was in distress, I sought the Lord;*
> *at night I stretched out untiring hands*
> *and my soul refused to be comforted.*

> [3]*I remembered you, O God, and I groaned;*
>   *I mused, and my spirit grew faint.*   Selah

> [4]*You kept my eyes from closing;*
>   *I was too troubled to speak.*
> [5]*I thought about the former days,*
>   *the years of long ago;*
> [6]*I remembered my songs in the night.*
>   *My heart mused and my spirit inquired:*

> [7]*"Will the Lord reject forever?*
>   *Will he never show his favor again?*
> [8]*Has his unfailing love vanished forever?*
>   *Has his promise failed for all time?*
> [9]*Has God forgotten to be merciful?*
>   *Has he in anger withheld his compassion?"*   Selah

> [10]*Then I thought, "To this I will appeal:*
>   *the years of the right hand of the Most High."*
> [11]*I will remember the deeds of the LORD;*
>   *yes, I will remember your miracles of long ago.*
> [12]*I will meditate on all your works*
>   *and consider all your mighty deeds.*

¹³*Your ways, O God, are holy.*
   What god is so great as our God?
¹⁴*You are the God who performs miracles;*
   you display your power among the peoples.
¹⁵*With your mighty arm you redeemed your people,*
the descendants of Jacob and Joseph.   Selah

¹⁶*The waters saw you, O God,*
   the waters saw you and writhed;
   the very depths were convulsed.
¹⁷*The clouds poured down water,*
   the skies resounded with thunder;
   your arrows flashed back and forth.
¹⁸*Your thunder was heard in the whirlwind,*
   your lightning lit up the world;
   the earth trembled and quaked.
¹⁹*Your path led through the sea,*
   your way through the mighty waters,
   though your footprints were not seen.

²⁰*You led your people like a flock*
   by the hand of Moses and Aaron. (Psalm 77)

STUDY

1. This psalm is divided into two segments: verses 1-9 and 10-20. What theme or themes do you see in each segment?

2. The psalmist writes about emotional and spiritual distress. How does he describe his experience of emotional distress?

3. How does the psalmist describe his experience of spiritual distress?

---

4. The psalmist says that his soul refuses to be comforted. Have you ever had an experience like this? What happened?

---

5. One reason the psalmist refuses to be comforted is that he is afraid that he has been abandoned or rejected by God. If you put yourself in the psalmist's place, what would it be like to fear that this is true?

---

6. In a time of quiet, ask God to show you any lack of hope you might have about the availability of God's comfort. Write whatever comes to mind.

---

7. In the second segment of this psalm, the psalmist makes a deliberate choice to remember God's loving actions on his behalf in the past—to remember who God is. What does the psalmist remember about God?

8. How can remembering the acts of God in the past help us move from refusing comfort to being open to comfort?

---

9. In a moment of quiet, ask God to help you remember evidence of God's loving presence in your life. Take a few minutes to reflect on whatever evidence comes to mind. Thank God for this evidence that you are loved, that you are valuable and that you are not alone. Ask God to let these memories open your heart to receiving comfort.

REFLECT

Spend some additional time asking God to help you remember times when you have been comforted by God or through others. Write a letter of thanks to God for these experiences.

RESPOND

Ask God to show you each day if there are fears that keep you from receiving comfort. Ask God to heal these fears. Keep a journal of whatever you sense God is showing you.

3

When Comfort Is Not Comforting

JOB 16:1-5, 18-21

Not all attempts to comfort are comforting. Many of us have experienced this. In times of loss we have experienced people speaking too soon, speaking too glibly about "all things working together for good," or offering advice about how to solve our problems. As a result, many of us have been shamed for our grief or distress. Henri Nouwen provides a helpful summary of the qualities that make comfort genuinely helpful:

> When we honestly ask ourselves which persons in our lives mean the most to us, we often find that it is those who, instead of giving much advice, solutions, or cures, have chosen rather to share our pain and touch our wounds with a gentle and tender hand. The friend who can be silent with us in a moment of despair or confusion, who can stay with us in an hour of grief and bereavement, who can tolerate not-knowing, not-curing, not-healing and face with us the reality of our powerlessness, that is the friend who cares. (*Out of Solitude* [Notre Dame, Ind.: Ave Maria Press, 1974], p. 34)

In the text for this study we find Job in a place where he needed the strength and hope that only comfort can give. Instead, he had to explain to his friends why their responses were not helpful. In the process of explaining what he needed, Job offers some insights about comfort that is genuinely comforting.

PREPARE

Think of a time when you needed comfort from another human being. What would have been comforting to you at the time?

Think of a time when you felt shamed rather comforted. What was this experience like?

 READ

¹Then Job replied:
  ² "I have heard many things like these;
    miserable comforters are you all!
³ Will your long-winded speeches never end?
  What ails you that you keep on arguing?
⁴I also could speak like you,
  if you were in my place;
I could make fine speeches against you
  and shake my head at you.
⁵But my mouth would encourage you;
  comfort from my lips would bring you relief. . . .

¹⁸ "O earth, do not cover my blood;
  may my cry never be laid to rest!
¹⁹Even now my witness is in heaven;
  my advocate is on high.
²⁰My intercessor is my friend
  as my eyes pour out tears to God;
²¹on behalf of a man he pleads with God
  as a man pleads for his friend." (Job 16:1-5, 18-21)

STUDY

1. If you were writing a newspaper article based on these verses, what headline would you use?

---

2. What is Job saying to his friends about their efforts to be helpful?

---

3. Put yourself in Job's place. What would it be like to have friends respond in this way to your need for comfort?

---

4. What kinds of words or actions are likely to be shaming rather than comforting?

---

5. It has been suggested that Job's friends were trying to play God in his life. They assumed that they had all the right answers and explanations for why Job was suffering. They were also playing God when they assumed that they were commissioned to tell Job what he was doing wrong. They were acting as if they knew all and as if they had the wisdom to judge another person's life. What fears or beliefs might be driving Job's friends to play God?

6. Think of a time when you might have responded like Job's friends to someone who needed comforting. How might it have helped you to let God be God at that time?

7. What would it be like to fear that God will respond to you with shame when you need comfort?

8. In verse 5 Job says that he would offer words of encouragement to someone in need of comfort. What words have you found encouraging?

9. Look at verse 18. What is Job saying here about what is comforting to us when we are distressed?

10. In verses 19-21 Job says that he needs someone to intercede for him with God as a man pleads for a friend. What about this would be comforting?

11. Job wants his friends to comfort him rather than shame him by acknowledging his suffering, speaking words of encouragement, and responding with care and compassion. What would it be like to know that God does not shame us when we are in distress but, instead, responds to our distress in all these ways?

---

12. In a moment of quiet, be aware that God wants to truly comfort you. Write a prayer telling God about whatever distress you need God to see and hear.

REFLECT

Read Hebrews 4:14-16. This text is a promise that God will not shame us when we need comfort. Allow these words to sink into your heart and mind as you read them two or three times. Write your response to this time of reflection.

RESPOND

Ask God to show you each day this week any fears you have about being shamed when you need comfort. Focus on the image in Hebrews 4:14-16 of being able to run to God whenever you need comfort without fear of being shamed. Keep a journal of whatever you sense God is showing you about your fears and about his compassion and understanding.

4

Asking God for Comfort

PSALM 31

We have seen in earlier studies that God wants to comfort us. In this study we turn our attention to asking God for comfort. When we ask God to comfort us, we are asking God to do what God already longs to do. But asking God to comfort us may not yet come easily. We may fear that God will blame us, shame us, ignore us or abandon us instead of comfort us. As we move through our fears and take the risk to ask, we open our hearts to receive. In the text for this study we will find some helpful guidelines for asking God for comfort when we need it most.

PREPARE
When you think of God comforting you, what images come to mind?

What experiences (satisfying or disappointing) have you had of asking God for comfort?

READ
¹In you, O LORD, I have taken refuge;
  let me never be put to shame;

deliver me in your righteousness.
²Turn your ear to me,
   come quickly to my rescue;
be my rock of refuge,
   a strong fortress to save me.
³Since you are my rock and my fortress,
      for the sake of your name lead and guide me.
⁴Free me from the trap that is set for me,
      for you are my refuge.
⁵Into your hands I commit my spirit;
   redeem me, O LORD, the God of truth.

⁶I hate those who cling to worthless idols;
   I trust in the LORD.
⁷I will be glad and rejoice in your love,
      for you saw my affliction
      and knew the anguish of my soul.
⁸You have not handed me over to the enemy
      but have set my feet in a spacious place.

⁹Be merciful to me, O LORD, for I am in distress;
      my eyes grow weak with sorrow,
      my soul and my body with grief.
¹⁰My life is consumed by anguish
      and my years by groaning;
my strength fails because of my affliction,
      and my bones grow weak.
¹¹Because of all my enemies,
   I am the utter contempt of my neighbors;
I am a dread to my friends—
      those who see me on the street flee from me.
¹²I am forgotten by them as though I were dead;
   I have become like broken pottery.
¹³For I hear the slander of many;
      there is terror on every side;
they conspire against me
      and plot to take my life.

¹⁴But I trust in you, O LORD;
   I say, "You are my God."
¹⁵My times are in your hands;

deliver me from my enemies
and from those who pursue me.
[16]Let your face shine on your servant;
save me in your unfailing love.
[17]Let me not be put to shame, O Lord,
for I have cried out to you;
but let the wicked be put to shame
and lie silent in the grave.
[18]Let their lying lips be silenced,
for with pride and contempt
they speak arrogantly against the righteous.

[19]How great is your goodness,
which you have stored up for those who fear you,
which you bestow in the sight of men
on those who take refuge in you.
[20] In the shelter of your presence you hide them
from the intrigues of men;
in your dwelling you keep them safe
from accusing tongues.

[21]Praise be to the Lord,
for he showed his wonderful love to me
when I was in a besieged city.
[22]In my alarm I said,
"I am cut off from your sight!"
Yet you heard my cry for mercy
when I called to you for help.
[23]Love the Lord, all his saints!
The Lord preserves the faithful,
but the proud he pays back in full.
[24]Be strong and take heart,
all you who hope in the Lord. (Psalm 31)

Study

1. What two or three themes do you see weaving in and out of this psalm?

2. How does the psalmist describe his distress?

3. What part of this description do you relate to?

4. List all of the requests that the psalmist makes of God.

5. List all of the actions the psalmist describes God taking on his behalf.

6. What does this psalm tell us about God?

7. What do you find comforting about the God who is described in this psalm?

8. Which of the requests that the psalmist made do you want to make to God?

---

9. Reflect during a few minutes of quiet prayer on the images of "strong fortress" and "rock of refuge." Let yourself experience the comfort of God—as God holds you, providing you with a strong fortress and a rock of refuge. Write about your experience during this time of prayer.

---

10. Write a brief prayer, thanking God for the comfort he is giving you.

REFLECT

In verse 16 of this psalm the psalmist says, "Let your face shine on your servant; save me in your unfailing love." Spend some time reflecting on this image of God's face shining on you. Spend some time reflecting on God's unfailing love. Write whatever response you have to this verse.

RESPOND

Each day this week, ask God for comfort. Whether you are in distress or having a good day, ask for God's comfort in specific ways. Notice any hesitation you might have to asking. Keep a written record of your requests, your experience of asking and the ways you sense God is responding to your requests.

5

Receiving
God's Comfort

ISAIAH 40:9-11

Giving and receiving comfort is an intimate exchange. Comfort is not a feature of contractual or economic relationships. It is not a commodity. It can't be purchased or sold. It is a quality of relationship that requires (and is made possible by) emotional closeness. Receiving comfort can only happen when the person offering comfort and the person receiving comfort are emotionally close.

The Bible is quite clear that the kind of relationship that God wants to have with us is characterized by emotional closeness. The God of the Bible is not the unmoved Mover who starts things off and then leaves everything to run by itself. The God of the Bible is moved by our experiences, reaches out to us in active love and longs for a relationship with us which is characterized by trust, closeness and affection. God offers comfort to us in the context of a loving relationship.

It is possible that we are not accustomed to thinking of God in such intimate, caring terms. Yet the text for this study, along with many other Scriptures, reveals a God who is both powerful and close enough to us to provide comfort.

PREPARE
What benefits have you experienced as a result of receiving comfort from others?

What benefits have you experienced as a result of receiving comfort from God?

READ

⁹You who bring good tidings to Zion,
*   go up on a high mountain.*
You who bring good tidings to Jerusalem,
* lift up your voice with a shout,*
lift it up, do not be afraid;
* say to the towns of Judah,*
* "Here is your God!"*
¹⁰See, the Sovereign LORD comes with power,
* and his arm rules for him.*
See, his reward is with him,
* and his recompense accompanies him.*
¹¹He tends his flock like a shepherd:
* He gathers the lambs in his arms*
and carries them close to his heart;
* he gently leads those that have young. (Isaiah 40:9-11)*

STUDY

1. This passage begins by saying it is a declaration of good tidings. What are the good tidings in this text?

2. In what ways is God's power important to you when you need comfort?

3. How do the images of God as powerful in this text compare or contrast to your expectations of God?

4. Take a few minutes of quiet to put yourself into this passage and experience God as a powerful ruler. Allow yourself to receive comfort from God, the loving, powerful ruler. Write about your experience in this time of reflection.

5. In what ways is God's tender, loving presence important to you when you need comfort?

6. How do the images of God as tender Shepherd compare or contrast to your expectations of God?

7. Take a few minutes of quiet to put yourself into this passage and experience God as a tender shepherd. Allow yourself to receive comfort from God the tender shepherd. Write about your experience in this time of reflection.

8. How have you experienced God's comfort during the time you have been doing these studies?

9. What comfort (help, strength, hope or consoling) do you need from God at this time?

REFLECT

Spend some time reading and reflecting on Psalm 23. Notice God has many ways of providing comfort. Write whatever response you have to this reflection.

RESPOND

Each day this week, spend a few minutes of quiet with God. Use the meditative prayer in questions 4 and 7 as you ask God to comfort you. Keep a daily journal of your experiences of receiving comfort from God.

6

Living in God's Comfort

2 CORINTHIANS 1:3-4

What happens when we let God be the God of comfort—when we let God comfort us? Our anxieties and fears are reduced. Our capacity for hope increases. Our capacity for joy increases. And we begin to experience gratitude again. Often in this gratitude we find the genesis of a desire to share what we have received. The experience of receiving comfort creates in us a desire to comfort others. Comfort is one of those valuable things that is not diminished at all by being given away.

In the text for this study we will see that we are "letting God be God" both by receiving comfort in our time of need and by sharing this comfort with others.

PREPARE
Think of a person who has been a safe and reliable source of comfort for you. What words would you use to describe this person?

What experiences have helped you to become a safer and more reliable source of comfort for others?

READ

³Praise be to the God and Father of our Lord Jesus Christ, the Father of compassion and the God of all comfort, ⁴who comforts us in all our troubles, so that we can comfort those in any trouble with the comfort we ourselves have received from God. (2 Corinthians 1:3-4)

STUDY

1. What title would you give this text?

2. These verses tell us that God, who is the Father of Jesus, is the Father of compassion. What images come to mind when you think of a compassionate father?

3. What images come to mind when you think of a compassionate God?

4. The text also tells us that God is the God of all comfort. What images come to mind when you think of a God of comfort?

5. In a moment of quiet, let God remind you that he is your Father who feels deep compassion for you and that he is the God of all comfort who wants to comfort you. Write about your experience in this time of prayer.

6. The text tells us that God comforts us in all our troubles. As we saw in an earlier study, when we are experiencing troubles we sometimes are afraid that God has forgotten us or rejected us. This text says that God is with us in all our troubles, offering us comfort. How might remembering this fact change how you experience times of trouble?

7. Recall a time of trouble in the past during which you thought you had been abandoned by God. What difference might it make to know that God was with you then?

8. Bring to mind fears that you have about the future. What comfort would it give you to know that the God of compassion and comfort will be with you in those times?

9. The text suggests that when we receive God's comfort we may become able to comfort others in the same way that God has comforted us. Think of an example of a time when you were able to comfort someone else. What was this experience like for you?

---

10. As you reflect on the ways God has comforted you, what would you like to do to be an instrument of God's comfort to others?

REFLECT
Spend some time reflecting on the names for God in this text: "The Father of compassion" and "The God of comfort." Ask God to show you more deeply and fully his compassion and comfort. Allow yourself to receive God's compassionate, comforting presence in this moment.

RESPOND
This text begins with praise. It is an expression of gratitude to God for who God is. It is an expression of thankfulness for how God comforts us and for the ways God allows us to comfort others. Write your own expression of praise and gratitude to God for the gift of comfort and for the ways you have been able to comfort others.

Leader's Notes

You may be experiencing a variety of feelings as you anticipate leading a group through this study guide. You may feel inadequate for the task and afraid of what will happen. If this is the case, know you are in good company. Many other small group leaders share this experience. It may help you to know that your willingness to lead is a gift to the other group members. It might also help if you tell them about your feelings and ask them to pray for you. Realize as well that the other group members share the responsibility for the group. And realize that it is the Spirit's work to bring insight, comfort, healing and recovery to group members. Your role is simply to provide guidance to the discussion. The suggestions listed below will help you to provide that guidance.

Preparing to Lead

1. Develop realistic expectations of yourself as a small group leader. Do not feel that you have to "have it all together." Rather, commit yourself to an ongoing discipline of honesty about your own needs. As you grow in honesty about your own needs, you will grow as well in your capacity for compassion, gentleness and patience with yourself and with others. As a leader you can encourage an atmosphere of honesty by being honest about yourself.

2. Pray. Pray for yourself. Pray for the group members. Invite the Spirit to be present as you prepare and as you meet.

3. Read the text several times.

4. Take your time to thoughtfully work through each question, writing out your answers.

5. After completing your personal study, read through the leader's notes for the study you are leading. These notes are designed to help you in several ways. First, they tell you the purpose the authors had in mind while writing the study. Take time to think through how the questions work together to accomplish that purpose. Second, the notes provide you with additional background information or comments on some of the questions. This information can be useful when people have difficulty understanding or answering a question. Third, the leader's notes can alert you to potential problems you may encounter during the study.

6. If you wish to remind yourself during the group discussion of anything mentioned in the leader's notes, make a note to yourself below that question in your study guide.

Leading the Study

1. Begin on time. You may want to open in prayer, or have a group member do so.

2. Be sure everyone has a study guide. Decide as a group whether you want people to do the study on their own ahead of time. If your time together is limited, it will be helpful for people to prepare in advance.

3. At the beginning of your first time together, explain that these studies are meant to be discussions, not lectures. Encourage the members of the group to participate. However, do not put pressure on those who may be hesitant to speak during the first few sessions. Clearly state that people do not need to share anything they do not feel safe sharing. Remind people that it will take time to trust each other.

4. Read aloud the group guidelines listed in the front of the guide. These commitments are important in creating a safe place for people to talk and trust and feel.

5. Read aloud the introductory paragraphs at the beginning of the discussion for the day. This will orient the group to the passage being studied.

6. If the group does not prepare in advance, approximately ten minutes will be needed for individuals to work on the "Prepare" section. This is designed to help group members focus on some aspect of their personal experience. Hopefully it will help group members to be more aware of the frame of reference and life experience that we bring to the text. This time of personal reflection can be done prior to the group meeting or as the first part of the meeting. The prepare questions are not designed to be for group discussion, but you might begin by asking the group what they learned from the prepare questions.

7. Read the passage aloud. You may choose to do this yourself, or someone else may read if he or she has been asked to do so prior to the study.

8. As you begin to ask the questions in the guide, keep several things in mind. First, the questions are designed to be used just as they are written. If you wish, you may simply read them aloud to the group. Or you may prefer to express them in your own words. However, unnecessary rewording of the questions is not recommended.

Second, the questions are intended to guide the group toward understanding and applying the main idea of the study. The authors of the guide have stated the purpose of each study in the leader's notes. You should try to understand how the study questions and the biblical text work together to lead the group in that direction.

There may be times when it is appropriate to deviate from the study guide. For example, a question may have already been answered. If so, move on to the next question. Or someone may raise an important question not covered in the guide. Take time to discuss it! The important thing is to use discretion. There may be many routes you can travel to reach the goal of the study. But the easiest route is usually the one the authors have suggested.

9. Don't be afraid of silence. People need time to think about the question before formulating their answers.

10. Don't be content with just one response. Ask, "What do the rest of you think?" or "Anything else?" until several people have given answers to the question.

11. Acknowledge all contributions. Try to be affirming whenever possible. Never reject an answer. If it seems clearly wrong to you, ask: "Which part of the text led you to that conclusion?" or "What do the rest of you think?"

12. Don't expect every answer to be addressed to you, even though this will probably happen at first. As group members become more at ease, they will begin to interact more effectively with each other. This is a sign of a healthy discussion.

13. Don't be afraid of controversy. It can be very stimulating. Differences can enrich our lives. If you don't resolve an issue completely, don't be frustrated. Move on and keep it in mind for later. A subsequent study may resolve the problem.

14. Stick to the passage under consideration. It should be the source for answering the questions. Discourage the group from unnecessary cross-referencing. Likewise, stick to the subject and avoid going off on tangents.

15. Periodically summarize what the group has said about the topic. This helps to draw together the various ideas mentioned and gives continuity to the study. But be careful not to use summary statements as an opportunity to give a sermon!

16. End each study with a prayer time. You will want to draw on the themes of your study and individual prayer and meditation as you now pray together. There are several ways to handle this time in a group. The person who leads each study could lead the group in a prayer, or you could allow time for group participation. Remember that some members of your group may feel uncomfortable about participating in public prayer. It might be helpful to discuss this with the group during your first meeting and to reach some agreement about how to proceed.

Listening to Emotional Pain

These Bible study guides are designed to take seriously the pain and struggle that is part of life. People will experience a variety of emotions during these studies. Part of your role as group leader will be to listen to emotional pain. Listening is a gift that you can give to a person who is hurting. For many people it is not an easy gift to give. The following suggestions will help you to listen more effectively to people in emotional pain.

1. Remember that you are not responsible to take the pain away. People in helping relationships often feel that they are being asked to make the other person feel better. This is usually related to the helper's own anxiety about painful feelings.

2. Not only are you not responsible to take the pain away, but one of the things people need most is an opportunity to face and to experience the pain in their life. They may have spent years denying their pain and running from it. Healing can come when we are able to face our pain in the presence of someone who cares about us. Rather than trying to take the pain away, then, commit yourself to listening attentively as it is expressed.

3. Realize that some group members may not feel comfortable with others' expressions of sadness or anger. You may want to acknowledge that such emotions are uncomfortable but that part of the growth process is to learn to feel and allow others to feel.

4. Be very cautious about giving answers and advice. Advice and answers may make you feel better or competent, but they may also minimize peoples' problems and their painful feelings. Simple solutions rarely work, and they can easily communicate "You should be better now" or "You shouldn't really be talking about this."

5. Be sure to communicate direct affirmation any time people talk about their painful emotions. It takes courage to talk about our pain because it creates anxiety for us. It is a great gift to be trusted by those who are struggling.

Study Notes
The following notes refer to the questions in the Bible study portion of each study.

Study 1. The Promise of Comfort. Isaiah 61:1-3.
Purpose: To hear God's promise of comfort.

Question 1. The purpose of this question is to help participants look at the text from a broad perspective. Welcome a variety of titles.

Question 2. God is reaching out to the poor, brokenhearted, captives, prisoners and those who grieve.

Question 3. Encourage people to look at these categories as having physical, emotional and spiritual characteristics. People may find themselves relating to more than one situation. If they do not relate to any of these categories, ask them if there has been a time in their life when they experienced a distressing time similar to those listed.

Question 4. The comforting actions which are promised are the preaching of good news, the binding up of broken hearts, the proclamation of freedom, release from darkness and comforting.

Question 5. This text reveals a God who knows our situation, has compassion for us and acts in powerful ways on our behalf to heal, free and comfort us. Our personal experience of God may, however, be quite varied. Even people who are deeply committed Christians may experience times in life when God's comfort seems impossibly distant. Encourage people to share honestly their current experience of God.

Question 6. The images of comforting are very powerful in this text. The promise to people who are grieving and in need of comfort from God is that they will be crowned in beauty, anointed with the oil of gladness and clothed in garments of praise. Beauty, gladness and praise will replace the heavy despair of grief.

Question 7. Allow participants three to five minutes to reflect on these images of comfort, to hear God promising them these powerful personal gifts of comfort and to write about their reflections. Then invite group members to share some of what they have written. Help group members to realize they will each have unique responses, depending on many things, including how they are feeling physically at the moment, the particular emotional stresses they are experiencing, and how safe they may or may not feel in this group. Encourage people not to judge themselves for their ability or inability to take in the reality of God's promise of comfort.

Question 8. You may want to let participants read the text in this way quietly to themselves, or you may want to give them an opportunity to read it aloud to the group. For example, "Joan will be called an oak of righteousness, a planting of the LORD for the display of his splendor." Take some time for people to share their response to God's promise to them.

Question 9. As the group leader, you may want to begin this time by sharing briefly from your experience. The model you set for vulnerability and honesty will have a large effect on how comfortable people will be in sharing their own needs. You might want to let participants write for a minute or two about something they want to share so everyone has some time to reflect on what they want to say. If time is limited, you will need to make that clear and give each person equal time to share.

Study 2. Refusing God's Comfort. Psalm 77.

Purpose: To be aware of times when receiving God's comfort is difficult.

Question 1. The purpose of this question is to provide an overview of the text. There are several ways to state the major themes. Encourage people to describe in their own words how they would state these themes. A basic version might be (1) despair and (2) hope. Or (1) when there is no comfort and (2) hoping for comfort.

Question 2. Encourage group members to examine the text to understand the psalmist's experience. On an emotional level he is groaning and is unable to sleep or speak.

Question 3. On a spiritual level the psalmist feels abandoned by God. Even though he calls and calls to God, it seems that God does not respond.

Question 4. As the group leader you might want to be prepared to share briefly and personally about such a time in your own life. Refusing to be comforted may come at a time when we are too angry or too distraught over something that has happened. Or we may be in shock. Or we may feel that receiving comfort is somehow a minimizing of a terrible situation. There are many reasons we may feel this way.

Question 5. This may be one of the most painful and frightening things we can feel as humans. We are God's creatures, and consciously or unconsciously, we all actively seek a relationship with God. If we feel abandoned or rejected by God, it is a devastating blow to our core identity as creatures, and it will be very difficult to sustain hope.

Question 6. Give group members time to pray and reflect alone. If you want, and the group is open to doing so, you can allow time for people to share whatever they want about this exercise.

Question 7. The psalmist remembers the powerful drama of the exodus. It was an event that was remembered and celebrated to provide hope in times when things seemed hopeless. In a similar way, Christians celebrate and remember God's powerful act of love in the death and resurrection of Jesus.

Question 8. This kind of remembering can help us in times when it seems that all hope is gone. As we remember God's care for us in the past, we grow in our ability to receive comfort and hope. Reflecting on God's acts of love can increase our hope that we will receive what we are seekin, or that what God provides will meet our needs in ways that we have not yet imagined. This is what the psalmist did in this text. Remembering times of comfort from God or hearing other people's experiences of God's comfort can also increase our hope and our willingness to ask for comfort.

Question 9. Give group members time to pray and reflect alone. If you want, and the group is open to doing so, you can allow time for people to share whatever they experienced during this exercise.

Study 3. When Comfort Is Not Comforting. Job 16:1-5, 18-21.

Purpose: To explore the characteristics of true comfort by distinguishing comforting words and behaviors from shaming words and behaviors.

Question 1. The purpose of this question is to help participants look at the text from a broad perspective. Welcome a variety of titles.

Question 2. Job is telling his friends that they are making long speeches and endless arguments. They are approaching his suffering from the neck up. This intellectualizing keeps them emotionally distant. Job also says that the speeches which they are making are against him and not for him. They are shaking their heads at him. They are judging him and shaming him for his suffering. They are telling him that he brought this suffering on himself; he deserves this distress.

Question 3. This kind of intellectualized, judgmental response is deeply shaming. It would leave any of us angry and despairing.

Question 4. Anything we do that allows us to remain emotionally distant from another person's suffering will leave that person feeling exposed and alone. This creates shame and despair—just the opposite of the strength and hope that comes from comfort. Encourage group members to reflect on words and actions that keep us emotionally distant from one another's suffering.

Question 5. Why did Job's friends behave this way? And why are similar behaviors so common today? It is possible that the behavior of Job's friends was driven by fears about God. They may have feared that God was a stern judge. They may have feared that they would meet the same fate as Job. If we have these kinds of fears and we can explain why another person is suffering, then maybe we will be able to convince ourselves that we are immune from such suffering. If we convince ourselves that we aren't as bad as other people, maybe we don't need to be so afraid. Fears about being incompetent, out of control or helpless can also lead to these kinds of behaviors. Such fears often lead us to work overtime to seem competent and in control. We may also fear that we are supposed to be able to come up with answers and keep other people in line. Each of these fears are related to fears about God and about ourselves.

Question 6. When we try to play God, we get overwhelmed and stressed. It is a job that is way too big for us. On the other hand, when we are able to sustain the humility of knowing that there is much we do not know and that we are truly not in control of much that happens in life, we are freer to be fellow creatures and sufferers with those who are in distress. And we are freer to allow others to be there for us when we are in distress. The result is that we are able to experience deeper connection and intimacy with others. Rather than moving away from other people when they are in pain or distress, we are able to move close. The cost is that we will feel pain. We will taste some of their distress. We will experience our helplessness and our longing for God's intervention on their behalf.

Question 7. Many people are afraid that God will be like Job's friends and respond with judgment to suffering. Such fears cause us to withdraw from God, to feel we cannot go to God when we are in distress and need comfort.

Question 8. Words that are comforting are often very simple: "Tell me what happened." "How are you doing with this?" "I am so sorry you are going through this." "Thank you for talking to me about what you are experiencing." "I love you." These are words that allow us to be with a person in a time of distress and to experience that distress—and our powerlessness—with them.

Question 9. Our pain needs to be seen and heard. This need cannot be minimized. It is central to the experience of being comforted. We need a witness to our experience. We need to feel understood and loved in the midst of our distress. We are comforted when we know that someone sees and hears what we are suffering and has a respectful compassion for us.

Question 10. A friend is someone who hears and feels our suffering, someone who cares about what we are experiencing. Friends will move closer to us in times of trouble rather than distancing themselves. Friends are willing to face their own powerlessness, understanding that they are not God. And friends are people who are prepared to plead with God for us—letting God be God.

Question 11. Encourage participants to reflect on the difference it would make to trust that God would respond to them in these ways.

Question 12. Give group members time to reflect and pray alone. Then allow time for people to share their prayers in a time of group prayer.

Study 4. Asking God for Comfort. Psalm 31.

Purpose: To learn to ask for God's comfort.

Question 1. The psalmist was experiencing great distress as he wrote this psalm. The text jumps from one thing to the next and back again, as anyone would do when they are highly anxious. At least five themes emerge, including (1) the experience of fear and distress, (2) the psalmist's call to God for help, (3) a description of some of what is causing the distress, (4) a prayer for justice or fairness and (5) an expression of trust and gratitude for God's faithfulness and love.

Question 2. Encourage group members to look closely at the text for the many specific descriptions the psalmist makes of his distress.

Question 3. Allow some time for people to reflect on experiences they have had that are similar to that of the psalmist and to share about a time when they may have felt something similar to what the psalmist describes in this text.

Question 4. Again, encourage group members to look closely at the text for the specific requests the psalmist makes of God.

Question 5. Encourage group members to look closely at the text for the specific actions that the psalmist credits to God.

Question 6. The overall picture of God which emerges in this text is of a God who is good, loving and merciful, and actively involved in our lives. We can call out to God for help. We can count on God to hear us and to respond in love and power.

Question 7. Allow group members an opportunity to reflect personally on the comfort the psalmist receives from God and on the comfort they see as available from God.

Question 8. Participants may have other requests as well. Encourage people to take the step of asking for God's specific gifts of comfort.

Question 9. Give group members time to reflect on these images in personal ways and to write about their reflections. Make time for them to share what they want to share about their responses to these images of God.

Study 5. Receiving God's Comfort. Isaiah 40:9-11.

Purpose: To learn to receive God's comfort.

Question 1. The good tidings in this text are about God. They are about God's presence: "Here is your God!" They are about who God is: He "comes with power" and "he gathers the lambs in his arms."

Question 2. God's power is very significant when we are seeking comfort. God is not helpless in the face of our need. God can do what we cannot do for ourselves. Like a child relying on a parent's strength, wisdom and knowledge, we can rely on God.

Question 4. This study provides an opportunity to actively reflect on and receive God's comfort. The questions are designed with this in mind. Allow time for participants to spend time in individual prayer and reflection, and time for sharing their experiences with each other and praying with and for each other.

Question 5. God's power is very important to us when we need help and comfort. But equally important is God's gentle, patient, respectful tenderness. God's responses to us are personalized—based on God's intimate knowledge of our need and who we are.

Question 6. Encourage participants to share their personal responses to these images of God's tender love and comfort.

Question 8. This is an opportunity to review and celebrate some of what God's Spirit has been doing in the lives of group members.

Study 6. Living in God's Comfort. 2 Corinthians 1:3-4.

Purpose: To continue to receive God's comfort and to explore the possibility of comforting others.

Question 1. The purpose of this question is to help group participants look at the text from a broad perspective. Welcome a variety of titles.

Question 2. Group members may want to define and describe the word *compassionate*. They may want to describe someone they knew who was a compassionate father.

Question 3. It is important to give participants an opportunity to put the concepts of compassion and father together with the truth about who God is.

Encourage them to struggle honestly with this if it is not easy for them. Encourage them to take in this truth about God as much as they can.

Question 4. Encourage group members to share images (word pictures), such as images of being held by Jesus.

Question 5. Allow participants time for individual prayer and reflection so that they can personally open their hearts and minds more fully to this wonderful truth about God. They may need three to five minutes to reflect on this name for God, what it means to them and to write about their reflections.

Question 6. Perhaps the most painful kind of distress comes from the belief that we are alone in times of distress. Scripture teaches us that God is with us in all our times of trouble. There is no conditional clause in this statement. God comforts us in all of our troubles. We are not, we never have been and we never will be alone.

Question 7. Encourage participants to think of a specific time in the past when they felt alone, and then to reflect on the reality that God was with them.

God has always been with us, aware of our distress, offering us comfort. This is true even when we have felt abandoned by God. If we have experienced a season of God's "absence" we need not shame ourselves for this experience. Realizing that God was present in loving ways in that difficult time can help free us from the wound created by believing that we were alone.

Question 8. Often, when people think of the future and imagine difficulties, they do not also remember that God will be with them, providing all the help and comfort which will be needed. Encourage group participants to think of a specific fear associated with a future event and then to reflect on the truth that God will be with them should this event occur.

Question 9. It is often a deeply moving experience to be with someone in a time of distress. It is not necessarily an easy experience. Our instincts may be to protect ourselves or to distance ourselves from this experience. When we share the comfort we have received from God, we not only give strength and hope to another person, but in the process we often receive more strength and hope as well.

Question 10. God blesses and then gives us the joy of sharing the blessing. God comforts us and then gives us the deep satisfaction of offering the same comfort to others. Encourage group members to remember what responses are truly comforting and to struggle honestly with any ongoing fears of sharing another person's experience of distress.

Online Resources

If you would like to share your experience using this Bible study with other people, we invite you to join us online at

<www.lettinggodbegod.com>

At the website you will be able to sign up to receive a free daily meditation written by Dale and Juanita Ryan.

Additional resources of interest to some users of these studies can be found at the online home of the Ryans:

<www.christianrecovery.com>